COUNTRY LIVING

500
Kitchen Ideas

Style, Function & Charm

COUNTRY LIVING

500
Kitchen Ideas

Style, Function & Charm

From the Editors of
COUNTRY LIVING Magazine

Text by Dominique DeVito

HEARST BOOKS
A division of Sterling Publishing Co., Inc.

New York / London
www.sterlingpublishing.com

Cover design by Celia Fuller; interior design by Areta Buk/Thumb Print

Library of Congress Cataloging-in-Publication Data
DeVito, Dominique C.
Country living: 500 kitchen ideas : style, function and charm / from Dominique DeVito and the editors of *Country Living* magazine.
p. cm.
Includes index.
ISBN 978-1-58816-695-1
1. Kitchens. 2. Interior decoration. I. Country Living (New York, N.Y.) II. Title. III. Title: 500 kitchens.
NK2117.K5D487 2008
747.7'97—dc22
2007047740

10 9 8 7 6 5 4 3 2 1

Published by Hearst Books
A Division of Sterling Publishing Co., Inc.
387 Park Avenue South, New York, NY 10016

Country Living and Hearst Books are trademarks of Hearst Communications, Inc.

www.countryliving.com

For information about custom editions, special sales, premium and corporate purchases, please contact Sterling Special Sales Department at 800-805-5489 or specialsales@sterlingpublishing.com.

Distributed in Canada by Sterling Publishing
c/o Canadian Manda Group, 165 Dufferin Street
Toronto, Ontario, Canada M6K 3H6

Distributed in Australia by Capricorn Link (Australia) Pty. Ltd.
P.O. Box 704, Windsor, NSW 2756 Australia

Manufactured in China

Sterling ISBN 978-1-58816-695-1

contents

introduction

Choosing the right style and look for your kitchen can be daunting—after all, it's the busiest room in the house and the one that offers the most options in terms of design, features, and storage. But don't look at it as a stressful undertaking. Instead, use the experience to find out things about yourself and your family, your daily life, and what will make the room function best to suit your specific needs. And, don't forget to surround yourself with the colors, collections, and modern-day conveniences that will improve your life and make the time spent in the kitchen more enjoyable.

All of the tips and ideas in this book were drawn from the pages of *Country Living* and selected to inspire and help you update your existing kitchen or successfully plan a new one. There are tips on working with color, pattern, and texture; choosing the best wall and floor coverings; finding the right cabinet style; optimizing space with built-in appliances and features; and a multitude of storage and display solutions for everything from basic utensils to treasured collections. I hope this book will inspire you to create the kitchen of your dreams.

—Nancy Mernit Soriano
Editor in Chief, *Country Living*

1

Highlight different wood finishes with a neutral palette of light colors. The distressed finish of the cabinets and island defines the farmhouse style of this kitchen.

2

Conceal appliances behind cabinets so the creamy color of the wood becomes the kitchen's predominating feature. Add a dark Windsor chair and a collection of dark brown pottery to contrast with the light palette.

3

Draw the eye with deep pigmented cabinets such as these. Painted black, then distressed, they provide a grounding visual element between the white marble counters and the richly grained floor.

4

The black-and-white-check fabric on the wing chair helps the kitchen's color scheme pop, as it plays off the black cabinets and white countertop and contrasts nicely against the yellow walls and gray window frames.

5

Give a kitchen appeal with interesting choices. Use the same dark wood normally found on floors for the ceiling or place formal stools that would more likely be seen in a dining room, by the island. Even add a colored door as a bold departure from a mostly white color scheme.

6

Make a narrow kitchen appear more spacious by painting only one side of the room a color and the other side white. In addition, a horizontally striped runner leads the eye from the kitchen into the next room—opening up the flow.

Temper colored cabinetry along one side of a kitchen with white countertops and serving pieces. Here, the white accents complement the cabinets along the right side of the kitchen.

8

Enliven an all-white kitchen with wall-paper that has a strong color, pattern—or both. Here the rooster-themed wallpaper with its black diamond background draws the eye to the far wall where light from a double window helps brighten the space.

Provide a neutral background for collectibles of all kinds with pastel colors. The soft greens and blues here that accentuate the pantry, transition nicely into the kitchen, where they are picked up again in subtle ways.

10

Make a pottery collection the colorful focal point of a kitchen by showcasing it on open shelves. The expansive assortment of blue-and-white-striped pottery sets the tone for this kitchen.

11

Consider using easily attainable objects such as flowers or fruit to bring different colors into your kitchen on a regular basis. Lemons and sunflowers are a simple way to bring bright yellow into this kitchen.

12

Too much pattern on a wall can dominate a space and make it seem smaller than it is. Here, only a portion of the wall is painted in alternating squares of pale blue, lavender, and soft yellow. The interplay of colors and shapes forms a playful, yet subdued pattern that is diverting but not distracting.

Showcase a collection of vintage china by painting the interior of a glass-fronted cabinet a color taken from the china itself. Here, bright rose picks up the various pinks in the floral patterns and provides a strong contrast to the white porcelain.

14

Before introducing a bold color into a small space, consider how to incorporate it. A corner cabinet with red-painted shelf interiors and front-door panels sets the tone for this compact but compelling space.

One important bright-colored piece is often all that's needed to add originality to a kitchen. Painted red, this island stands out against the white surfaces that surround it. Two open cabinets on the far wall are filled with books and pantry staples that add additional interest and color to the space.

16

Choosing to paint a portion of a wood cabinet in a soft shade expands the color palette of a room without being over-powering. The antiqued glaze finish on the front and sides of this cabinet contrasts with the warm wood of its well-polished countertop. The effect is soothing and harmonious.

17

Combine natural wood with painted surfaces to create a vibrant kitchen environment. A barn-red paint is used for the cabinet cases here while mustard-colored pine moldings accent the darker tone of the natural wood stiles and fields of the doors.

18

Use color to lead you from space to space. Here, a strong red stands alone to give character to the kitchen and it extends into the dining room to keep the color theme going. A bit of unexpected whimsy is introduced into the tableau by a classic toile wallpaper covered ceiling.

19

Finding appliances and other kitchen items that coordinate with your color scheme is no longer difficult. This kitchen has a bright red espresso maker, red canisters for sugar and such, red glassware, and more!

20

To satisfy a passion for a certain color without feeling overwhelmed by it, use it as a defining accent. Here, a tomato-red window frame sets the stage for other red items, including dishtowels and a collection of papier-mâché fruits.

21

To get the same colorful focal point without a window, hang a mirror in a red-painted frame above the sink. It will also make the room look larger.

22

If a strong color like red seems too daring, consider including it in accent pieces or collections. The red picked up in a variety of kitchen accessories here jazzes up the area with a vintage look.

23

If you're fortunate to have a vintage appliance or piece of furniture, take your color and decorating schemes from the object's accent color and mid-century design. In this case, the red accents on the stove are repeated in the selection of fifties-style kitchenware.

24

Keep color, shape, texture—and fun—in mind when designing your kitchen. There are few plain surfaces here. Raised and recessed angular designs decorate the cabinetry to balance the curved edges of the countertops. Hand-painted patterns are applied on nearly all surfaces and as busy as the scheme is, color pulls it all together.

25

Consistent elements are important in a space which has a lot of variation. Here, it's the overall tone of the colors. The muted palette of the various lavenders, yellow, greens, and whites helps create a cohesive look.

26

Accessorizing with color is a great way to feed your fancies. If you find something outrageously appealing—like these large, red paper flowers—and your kitchen is a neutral color overall, you can easily work it into the décor for a day, a week, a month, or as long as you like. When you tire of it, you can replace it with another found treasure that may inspire a new color scheme.

27

Transform an ordinary kitchen into a showstopper by using an unexpected color combination. In this space, lavender chairs and accessories complement sage green cabinets.

28

A retro table and chairs set the mood and tone for this funky kitchen. With lots of white to keep the room looking sparkling clean, this palette—green on the walls, the red enamel stove, turquoise canisters and other collectibles, and café curtains and braided rug that combine all these colors—unifies the areas of intense colors.

29

Primary colors make the vintage spirit of a small eat-in kitchen come alive. Dazzling yellow wall paint, a fifties dinette set with bright blue vinyl chairs, red touches on the vintage tablecloth, and stencils framing the window bring this kitchen back to life.

30

Make a bold statement by painting cabinets a bright color. Here, the turquoise sets a playful tone for an otherwise traditional country kitchen.

31

Install varying cabinets to make a huge difference in the overall appearance of your kitchen. Here, a set of white cabinets stands out against the lower yellow cabinets and refrigerator.

32

Adding shades of pale yellow, deep red, and bright blue, can make a kitchen feel like Provence, France, or Italy's Mediterranean coast. But here, the colors lend an Old World intimacy to an all-American country kitchen that incorporates a bun-footed dresser converted to a cabinet.

33

Decorating a country kitchen for the holidays is simple and easy. Work with the dominant colors in your kitchen and infuse the traditional green, red, and white as perfect accent colors. Miniature Christmas trees on the countertop; evergreen boughs, garlands, and ornaments on the hanging pot rack; and bowls of seasonal fruit make a festive and colorful backdrop to holiday preparations.

34

Paint cabinets a deep blue, add an earthy-red colored farmhouse table, or stain hardwood floors a golden-yellow to achieve a shaker-style look.

35

Add color and texture to a kitchen by choosing interesting flooring. Here, the most eye-catching element is the old plank floor that was painted to create a checkerboard pattern.

36

Mix traditional countertops, cabinets, rugs, or paintings with modern stainless appliances for a sleeker look. Silver and black complement each other very nicely.

37

Find ways to introduce colors you love into a space—such as the green antique painted chest and bright mustard vase and window trim here.

38

The combination of moss green and mustard yellow brings to mind the sun-dappled woods in many parts of the U.S. Here they are expertly paired to define this warm kitchen, with green framing the windows and covering the cabinets, and the yellow brought out in the wooden countertops, island top, and hanging ceiling lights.

39

Bring places you love to life with color. The ocher yellow here—in the paint color, the print upholstery and pillows, and the sun-inspired elements such as the pattern on the table, the chandelier, and, of course, the vase of sunflowers—gives one the feeling of being in Italy's Tuscan countryside.

40

Bright yellow walls and terra-cotta floor tiles infuse a room with warmth. Here, cool touches of blue—the wall hung antique cabinet, mismatched decorative plates, and quilt-draped armchair—balance the sunny colors.

41

Hang a message board in the busiest room of the house where notes and reminders will be seen by all. Make it stand out by placing it against a richly colored wall and positioning it in a particularly convenient spot.

42

Identify your kitchen's outstanding features and use color to show them off. Bring out the golden highlights of solid wood cabinets by painting the adjacent walls a dark blue.

43

Lean a colorful painting on a shelf over the sink to fill a large empty wall and complement the style of your kitchen. Here, the painting perfectly fits in with the collection of miniature farmhouses in this country kitchen.

44

Set the design tone for your kitchen by introducing cabinets with some different colors. Here, cherrywood drawers shine warmly against cabinets finished in a black-matte paint.

45

Paint woodwork a traditional Colonial blue to get the look of an early-American-style kitchen. Bring in period pieces to further accentuate the look.

46

Create a bold south-of-the-border ambience with vibrant Mexican hues of blue, orange, and yellow. Echo the colors and design of the backsplash tiles in the area rugs and display pieces for a truly authentic feeling.

47

Color helps transform extra wall space into a separate nook for prepping and storage. Hideaway doors painted the same pale blue as the rest of the room roll out to enclose the sink and cupboard when not in use. The effect: The built-ins magically disappear.

48

For a sense of fun and whimsy, consider unique colors and patterns for walls such as the blue-and-white checkerboard pattern here. Wedgwood blue cabinets and pale blue floors support the color theme.

49

The graphic pattern here is broken up by the placement of a stainless steel shelf and pot rack. The light island top and white ceiling keep the space from feeling too busy or claustrophobic.

50

Even with minimal wall space, color can have a dramatic impact. To give a mostly white kitchen some warmth, paint the walls a golden yellow.

51

Colorful accents bring a kitchen to life. Here, these thoughtful touches include pale yellow on the walls, black-and-white checkerboard flooring, natural wood doors and countertops, and a baby-blue enameled tin pail filled with white pumpkins.

52

A unit of open white cubbies perched on a simple white cabinet with multiple drawers offers roomy storage for everything from cookbooks to bottles of wine and colorful glassware. The items themselves also contribute additional colors, forms, and textures to the kitchen.

53

Make a kitchen cozy by introducing warm tones and natural materials. Here, the honey-colored butcher block countertops and light-oak island enhance the pale cabinets. Sun-baked terra-cotta floor tiles pull together the homey look.

54

Create a visually engaging wall by having a mixture of glass and wooden front cabinets. Items on display can be distinctive collections or everyday objects that bring color and shape to the space.

Make your kitchen distinctive with combinations of colors that work together—such as the mocha brown, bright white, and muted cream here.

56

An all-white kitchen is always bright, comfortable, and inviting. With its gorgeous hardwood floors polished and gleaming, this classic kitchen will make anyone feel at home.

57

Pick blinds that match the main color of your kitchen for an inconspicuous window covering. The white blinds on these windows are almost invisible against their surroundings and yet they are a versatile way to control the light in such a bright space.

58

The easiest way to experiment with light and tone is with paint. Typically, small wall areas can receive a variety of treatments. The choice here was to apply a very soft grayish blue to the areas not covered by white cabinets and tile backsplash.

59

A dark gray countertop is a great choice in an all white kitchen. Here, the color also works well with the grayish blue of the walls and small flowerpots on the windowsill.

60

Matching cabinet and countertop colors
will influence the overall flow of a space,
creating a clean and monochromatic look.
When you want to bring in another color,
small accents such as these yellow napkins
do the job.

61

Keep plates, bowls, and serving pieces all in the same color palette for a simple and stylish appearance. An open wood shelf is the perfect way to display such an appealing collection.

62

Pair black and white or dark and light for a classic and versatile color scheme. Simple objects like an empty frame as well as pots and pans with black cast-iron bottoms incorporate easily into the decorating plan.

Instead of tile, use beadboard as a back-splash for clean lines and easy cleanups. The white beadboard used here works nicely behind the modern stainless stove and flows well with the white cabinets.

64

Select milk paints in pale shades of mustard, cream and green to add depth and vitality to a large kitchen area. Along with the large skylight here, these colors contribute to the bright, airy feel of this kitchen.

65

Such a light, open space can support a darker color to ground it. The choice of dark green as an accent color for the couch and black wicker chairs, lamps, and other accessories adds substance, contrast, and depth to the multipurpose area.

66

The combination of painted and natural wood finishes creates a tastefully unique look. This principle is applied here with the rich cherrywood on the floor that also frames the custom-built island; the dark-blue painted wood of the display cupboard; and the white cabinets of the island.

Use color to unify spaces with numerous elements. For a small kitchen area like this, black, dark and light brown, and pale yellow work well together with the mix and match look. Painting the floor a decorative diamond pattern rather than keeping it one color also creates the illusion of a larger space.

68

Wallpaper can be a subtle but significant presence—such as the black-and-white check-patterned wallpaper in this kitchen that unifies the white cabinets and black work surfaces.

69

Think about the room adjacent to your kitchen when figuring out the color scheme. Here, there is a wonderful interplay between the colors in this group of rooms. A pale blue on the walls of the passageway leads to an even paler blue in the next room.

70

A dramatic architectural feature, such as the stone wall in this impressive space, can become the focus of a room and influence its color scheme. Here, the white walls, beamed ceiling, and woodwork enhance the stone's natural beauty.

71

Choose light wood for the island countertop, table, and chairs as a unifying element that completes a room and helps to make a large, open kitchen/dining area feel more intimate.

2 walls and floors

72

Join your kitchen and living space with similar elements. The clean white walls and antique wood beams here are carried over from the kitchen to the open living area. Also consider matching the floors in your kitchen with the hardwood in other areas of your home.

73

Take advantage of natural elements like an exposed brick chimney. The honey-colored wood countertops and two-tone cork tile floors work well with the large brick structure that is the focal point of the kitchen.

74

Get a sleek, modern feel using no-frills cabinets and soft shades of gray in your kitchen. A tall white pantry and a few decorative touches of black add to the minimalist design here.

75

For a visually appealing look, hang pots and pans of all shapes and sizes on hooks secured to beams that run along the wall rather than from the ceiling. Place them near appliances for convenience.

To keep a large space from looking too crowded, build shelves along the wall to store and showcase an abundance of kitchenware. Open shelves, racks for hanging cookware, and cabinets that are hung perpendicular to the wall supply additional storage space not found in standing cabinetry.

77

Large wooden posts and beams establish this kitchen's layout and ranch-house style. Hardwood floors in the same warm coloring, lots of natural light, and the country-style beadboard cabinetry contribute to the comfortable, down-home sensibility.

78

There is a refined grace in the simplicity of this kitchen. Gleaming hardwood floors and white walls provide a clean canvas on which to embellish—or not. The exposed brick surround of an old fireplace introduces a distinctive yet harmonious surface texture to the room.

79

Utilize a large butcher-block-style table as a center island when there are no wall cabinets or countertops for storage in part of your kitchen. You can place small appliances all along the table, ready to make quick use of the day's marketing.

80

Emulate an Adirondack lodge by bringing in elements such as the wide-beamed walls and hardwood floors here. For further effect, the wood has been stained and polished a golden color that brings both warmth and vitality.

Don't be afraid to cover many surfaces with wood. It's everywhere in this striking kitchen! Besides the wide beams on the walls, there is a gorgeous hardwood floor. The wood cabinets are painted a pale sage-green that complements yet contrasts with the warm natural hues all around.

82

To make your backsplash stand out, choose something different like this checkerboard one. Framed in reddish wood with matching shelves, the backsplash here adds flair against the black cabinets and white walls.

83

The signature look of a country kitchen is warm, rich wood. Here, the wide-planked floorboards and original beams set the tone for the dark wood cabinetry that provides an abundance of storage space and frames a pass-through, where items can be handed from the kitchen to the dining area.

84

To create a path from one room to the next, cover the floor between the kitchen and dining area with a homespun runner. This rug matches nicely with the dark wood cabinets, floors, beams, and pantry.

85

Maintain a comfortable country feel while updating your kitchen by replacing traditional rag rugs with new navy and white floor tiles. Cover the walls and ceiling with a blonde wood and add honey-stained cabinetry all around so the space isn't too dark.

86

Painting the radiator the same shade as the walls—such as the pale yellow color here—is a great alternative to getting a cover. This makes the radiator blend in rather than stand out.

87

Keep the country look of a remodeled kitchen by resurfacing the original cabinet doors with beadboard and adding butcher block counters. Here, light wood floors are painted with high-gloss enamel for smoothness and shine and soft yellow walls reflect the color choice of the vintage-style stove and fridge.

For additional storage space along otherwise unusable wall space, add a corner sideboard. This vintage blue one works well with the lively yellow-painted planked floor and ceiling.

89

Transform a sunroom into a dining area off of your kitchen by painting the hardwood floors a pale checkerboard pattern and extending it into the sunroom. This visually connects both rooms.

90

In an open plan where the kitchen and eating-and-sitting area are adjacent to each other, use graduating color on the floors, walls, and ceiling for a seamlessly blended appearance.

91

You can never have enough storage space in a kitchen, especially a small one. The floor-to-ceiling unit, waist-high cabinets, and hanging shelves here keep everything a busy kitchen needs right at hand. The pale cabinet color against the lustrous hardwood floor creates a well-defined, comfortable work area.

92

Maintain the integrity of a kitchen's style theme by incorporating major appliances into the design scheme. Here, a refrigerator is set in the wall flush between two pantries. For the large appliance to blend into the woodwork, the doors of the fridge should have the same finish as the pantry doors on either side.

93

Pair pale cabinets with similarly colored walls and floors to create a cool and comforting space. The mocha colored walls here, which have a stucco'd texture, complement the tiles and warm woodwork.

94

Pick up the color and texture of large wooden beams on the walls, cabinets, and flooring of your kitchen. The floor tiles here have the same weathered tone as the large beam that runs through this kitchen.

95

Finishing walls with a stucco effect complements the glazing technique used on the beams and all the wood pieces in this cottage kitchen.

96

Add nice texture to kitchen walls with small mosaic tiles. They are easy to keep clean, making them a very popular choice for backsplashes. This one, with white grouting, is of the same color as the old wooden beam used as a shelf and the antique earthenware that's stored on it.

One way to marry art and nature in a kitchen is to hang a large piece of art on an expansive stone wall. While both items complement each other in period and scale here, the gilt frame sharpens the stonework's neutral palette and the muted colors in the painting itself are used as accents in the room.

98

Walls help balance and define spaces—particularly large, open areas. Here, a half-wall island works triple-duty as a work surface, seating area, and room divider.

99

Use fieldstone and wood to retain the rustic feel of a log home—surround a large kitchen window with a stone arch instead of a traditional frame for a look reminiscent of an old-fashioned hearth.

100

A tall, two-storied pitched roof allows for a multitude of windows in place of solid walls. Here, three sides of windows flood the kitchen with natural light throughout the day and in all kinds of weather.

101

Figuring a structurally supportive beam into your decorating plan can be a challenge. Here, the beam is painted a pale blue like the rafters on the ceiling, which helps it blend in.

102

To complement almost any finish of wood, consider brick for your floors. The brick works in perfect harmony with the combination of cherrywood cabinets, the pale yellow woodwork, and even the white antique chest of drawers that's been converted to an island here.

103

Redefine a kitchen space by using stone on all major walls. Different finishes and styles are available and contrary to popular belief, range hoods and other objects can securely be hung from the stone.

104

To achieve a nineteenth-century look, add cherrywood cabinets, antique fir floorboards, and stained beadboard on the ceiling. Here, these rich woods are supplemented by an antique-reproduction oak island and an old farmhouse table. The wallpaper around the windows is a reproduction of a nineteenth-century pattern.

105

This large kitchen is outfitted with lots of storage space in cabinets and drawers that line the perimeter of the room. The refrigerator/freezer is hidden behind the tall cabinet on the right, which was custom built to match the other cabinetry.

106

The use of cherrywood from floor to ceiling throughout this kitchen infuses the room with a warmth that recalls the ambience of a friendly old tavern, inviting family and friends to linger.

107

Introduce colors of the sun and earth on the walls and floors for a cheerful kitchen—terra-cotta tiles and bright yellow paint are two ways to achieve this look.

108

Replace traditional cabinets under the sink with fabric for a real farmhouse feel. Three-quarter shutters on the picture window here are also a nice alternative to curtains on the walls.

109

Mix surface styles to create an interesting, eclectic look in a traditional kitchen. Here, linoleum intended for the floor becomes a practical, easy-care back-splash, and the sponge-painted finish on the range hood adds color where least expected.

110

As an alternative to paint, put bright blue-and white-patterned tiles on kitchen walls to ease the effect of dark elements such as floors, cabinets, and beams. Choose a tile pattern that supports the overall look and style of your kitchen.

111

A lot of heavy, dark wood in a kitchen can make the room seem smaller than it is. Have a wall of cabinets and shelves in a complementary medium tone to lighten the space. And with the walls just above and below the beams painted a very pale color here, the room doesn't feel closed in.

112

Turn a small space monopolized by a door and windows into a kitchen breakfast nook. A bench attached to the wall under the window is an inventive solution that puts wasted wall space to good use.

113

Wedgwood blue walls and multicolor parquet floors are traditional to a more formal setting. Yet in this cozy little corner they are right at home, paired with painted worn furniture, a flea-market chandelier, and blue-and-white china pieces hanging on the wall.

114

The nautical theme of this lakeside kitchen is played out in the slanted wood ceiling and large overhead beam that reminds one of a ship's cabin. The collection of model ships perched on the beam and the oval white platters above the windows, which look like portholes, accentuate the effect.

115

Fit a butcher block island such as this with an all-around curtain to keep the items on the shelves beneath out of sight. The vertical stripes of the fabric draw the eyes upward, toward the sloped ceiling.

116

When there is limited wall space between two architectural elements, such as a window and a door or two windows, it helps if you have an appliance or storage piece that fits right in. In this case, it's a coveted Aga stove.

117

Patterns help make a room inviting, and a popular checkerboard pattern instantly conveys a sense of familiarity and comfort. The pattern on this floor incorporates and balances scale, color, texture, and shape to achieve the desired result.

118

This summer-cottage kitchen is a good example of "salvage-style" decorating, where scruffy antique-store items, scraps of antique linens, even chipped china all become part of the décor. The two well-worn, mismatched hutches flanking the old-fashioned porcelain sink and double windows are flea-market finds. New wooden countertops give them life.

119

Bring instant sophistication to white cabinetry with slate-tiled floors. Also, beadboard on the ceiling is a great way to bring character to a kitchen.

Light floors let other features be the star—such as this all-blue island with a blue enamel sink. The hardwood floors here ensure that the island makes a statement.

121

A custom-made storage unit with cabinets, drawers, and glass-enclosed shelves is a wonderful use of wall space. Whitewashed from baseboard to ceiling and decorated sparsely, this kitchen is a cool and uncluttered place.

122

This space comes together through the marriage of blond wood and white surfaces. The floor and countertops keep the space grounded. The rest of the kitchen—appliances, walls, window frames—is white, giving a light-saturated lift to the room.

123

Doors should not be overlooked when decorating because they give the first impression of a home. That goes for the back door as well. This fire-engine red screen door with its gingerbread detailing seems an invitation to a very special place.

124

A pocket door conveniently closes off the entrance of this kitchen from the rest of the house. When the door is open, the painting connects the two rooms by reflecting the colors from the kitchen walls and limestone floor.

125

Fit an antique cabinet against a narrow wall. Here, it's a good use of wall space and also creates a shelf for a 1930s bread box and other enameled canisters.

126

Let the view from a large wall of windows inspire an outdoor-indoor design for flooring. In the work area, terra-cotta bricks have been laid to look like an outdoor terrace, ending where a gleaming hardwood floor begins. The junction of the two creates a natural division of space.

127

When wall space is mainly taken up by windows, mount a shelf above the oven's hood to store or display more items, such as the watering cans here.

128

In a room that has a lot of dark wood, as in this formal kitchen/dining room, using cool neutrals on the walls and cabinets is the best bet. Here, the purple hued walls and white cabinetry bring out the richness of the dark pieces.

129

Give a plain wood floor a new look with a painted faux finish. Here, the illusion of an opulent inlaid wood floor is created with nothing more than several colors of stain, a ruler, and a steady hand.

To add a dramatic personal statement to your kitchen, consider a one-of-a-kind mural made with hand-painted tiles. The center scene depicted here represents the owners' house, and the surrounding illustrations show it being built. But you can re-create any scenic landscape.

131

Preserve and utilize original beams as a decorative element when renovating your kitchen and figuring out the layout. Here, the main beam along the ceiling and far wall served as a good indicator for where the long countertop should be placed.

132

Don't cover up original walls if they work with the overall décor of your kitchen. Here, the plastered beam walls go with the hardwood floors and ceiling in the same hue.

133

This retro tile floor needs to take center stage! Keep the walls, fixtures, and furnishings neutral in their supporting role, and pick up the vibrant black in the countertop and backsplash to provide a dramatic backdrop.

134

Store a collection of serving pieces on open shelving so that their colors can complement and contrast with those of the walls and floors.

135

To add character to your kitchen, don't be afraid to cover walls with wallpaper such as the beautifully patterned leaf wallpaper here.

136

Natural stone floors can be a starting point for all other design choices in a kitchen. The rough faux-stone wall treatment here is a counterpoint to the floor's smooth surface, which is mirrored by a similarly dappled marble countertop and backsplash.

137

Well planned, bold mixes, can yield wonderfully unified results. Beadboard provides the common element between the stained wood island and the painted cabinets in this kitchen.

138

For an intimate dining niche, consider a built-in banquette. Here, the white walls and cream-colored panels of the built-in seating create the perfect atmosphere for family dining.

139

To add to the cozy feeling of an eating area like this, add earth-tone patterned pillows on the benches and soothing oil paintings above.

For a clean look, keep choices simple. Notice how the angular lines of this black chair stand out crisply against the white walls and golden hardwood floor. Such basic complementary elements open a world of decorating possibilities.

141

This stucco wall serves as a blank canvas: a textured backdrop for a changing display of favorite items, such as these stoneware platters. In this neutral-themed setting, the subtle dimensional surface of the stucco adds just enough visual stimulation to be interesting.

142

Decorative columns that extend from half walls or from floor to ceiling are an interesting design element. Here, the two columns separate the kitchen from the living space and their thicker bases provide even more distinction between the areas.

143

Distinct areas, each with their own designated purpose, can be forged out of an open space. A wall of sage green cabinets and a long cooktop/counter on a deep red wood base mark the boundaries of this kitchen. A dining area divides the kitchen from the family sitting room, and space under the window has been allotted for a small desk and window seat.

French doors and windows are framed in the same wood used throughout the kitchen and other areas. Left curtainless, they add interesting design details.

145

To carve out a small eating area from a functional kitchen, add walls and an archway to the space. The gray-green slate floor and hanging light fixtures visually connect the two areas.

146

Area rugs are both functional and visually appealing. Choose from different fabrics, patterns, sizes, and styles to fit in your kitchen.

147

Stain wood floors a dark chocolate brown for a timeless look. Here, the choice not only works well with the beadboard paneling covering the cabinets, but it makes for easy cleanup as well.

148

Architectural elements, such as picture molding on the walls and crown molding lining the ceiling, add character to any room. Molding does not have to be original to a home, in many cases the look can be achieved by putting up modern versions that look like they have been there for many years.

149

The geometry of kitchens—squares, rectangles, circles, and diamonds—plays out in appliances, cabinets, floors, and walls. This kitchen is designed to bring focus to these elements. The patterned tile floor with the decorative center is mirrored in the wall tiles as well as the Tiffany-inspired glass on the cabinet doors.

150

A neutral background of hardwood floors and white walls and cupboards is an ideal canvas for highlighting collections in the kitchen. White works well with everything, so even the most diverse collections or special items will show off nicely against it. Here, ample open shelving and glass-fronted cabinets are bursting with interesting collections of glassware, pottery, antique kitchen items, silver, and milk glass.

DELIGHTED

One of the most striking features of this space is the glazed pine floor. The light color sets the tone for the rest of the room, and is emphasized throughout by many accentuating touches. These include the chairs around the dining room table, the selection of similarly colored earthenware, and of course the wood that's used for the kitchen cabinets.

Make small spaces quite distinctive with different but harmonizing surface finishes. Here, the gleaming reddish brown laminated cabinets and boldly patterned linoleum floor work together to create a modern look.

153

A kitchen this open and light-filled easily supports a variety of wall colors and floor treatments. The smooth, warm wooden floor and bright walls convey an airy feel while darker floors, walls, or cabinets would create another aesthetic entirely.

154

The purity of this white kitchen forms a place of simple lines. The painted floorboards, walls, tall cupboard, table—even the white rug—help to create a space that is uncluttered and cheery.

155

Create an alfresco-like dining area between your kitchen and backyard by installing French doors in place of windows. For further effect, tile the floor with bluestone to simulate the look of an outdoor patio.

3 storage

156

Mount a cabinet in distressed condition on a stone wall to provide a beautiful, rustic storage space. The color blends perfectly with the old stone and emphasizes the brilliance of the white ironstone stored inside and on top.

157

Capitalize on ceiling height by installing tall cabinets and using the space on top to keep things in their place. Here, white ceramic pitchers line the top of the cabinets, keeping the collection in sight while not taking up useful cabinet space.

158

Because so much can accumulate around a sink, creative storage options needed to be introduced to keep the area clutter-free. These include large drawers to the left, a large and sturdy pot rack above the sink, and wall shelves for decorative platters.

159

An unique feature in this country kitchen is the use of old-fashioned hinges on the cabinets. They mirror the kinds of hinges found on the doors to extend the look all around. Wide wood panels on the cabinet fronts are also similar in look and feel to the old door.

160

Rather than enclose the space above the counters in your kitchen with cabinets, construct shelves to run the length of the walls. The strong horizontal lines of the open shelves are the dominant element in this kitchen and draw the eye up from the stove, sink, and dishwasher. Here, both everyday and decorative items find and share space.

Cabinets with clear glass doors contribute to an open and airy feeling in the kitchen. But often the contents don't merit the effort of maintaining a picture-perfect display, particularly in a busy, active household. Opt instead for translucent glass to gain this effect, and with the frosted finish, obscure any disorder on the shelves.

162

With exposed cabinets (either completely open or with glass fronts), presentation of the contents really matters and neatness does count. Display dishes of the same color scheme and arrange carefully. The overall look is balanced, and organized— a far cry from one of exposed clutter.

163

Even the simplest of storage choices can be transformed into a showcase. Here, two plain plank shelves have been painted pale green and mounted on white fretwork brackets.

164

Vintage collectibles find a home in this simple, open cabinet. The narrow, shallow unit with its pale smoke-blue interior, creates a lovely background to display glass mason jars and other similar small items.

An old screened pie cupboard serves multiple storage purposes. With open shelving above, a drawer in the middle, and the traditional screened cabinet, there are plenty of places to store things out in the open or hidden.

Scour flea markets and yard sales to find old pieces that can be given new lives as practical storage solutions. In this colorful kitchen, an old tool storage chest is transformed into a set of drawers for kitchen miscellany and a unit of cubbies that may have once held a classroom's supplies has been painted and given a sleek new top and mismatched handles to provide another unusual storage area.

167

Just because a window is present does not mean that display options cannot be incorporated. This glass shelf floating near the top of the window is a great airy platform for a glassware collection. The placement above eye level does not obstruct the beautiful view.

168

Simple storage options help a kitchen function more efficiently. A dish rack is a space-saving and attractive built-in to store plates at the ready. Jars are more decorative, but equally practical for storing frequently used staples.

169

Showcase a mixed collection of white ironstone and black-and-white transferware in a built-in cabinet with adjustable, open shelves. These shelves provide flexibility for storing pieces of various sizes.

170

This heavily distressed cabinet has been given a clean, new interior with wallpaper backing and well-waxed shelves. Fresh flowers and shells support the neutral colors and nature theme of the paper, and a compote dish of fresh cherries adds vibrancy to the monochromatic scheme.

An antique cupboard is a wonderful choice for holding a collection of various items. The stylized leaves hand painted on the drawers and the gracefully shaped brackets of this Welsh cupboard are charming reminders of our impulse to embellish even the most functional items in our homes.

172

An oversized countertop backsplash creates an ideal place for storing salt and pepper, oils and vinegars as well as other condiments used when cooking that would otherwise clutter the countertop.

173

Consider how storage decisions affect the symmetry of your kitchen. These two pot racks hang on both sides of the range hood, which not only offers double the amount of storage, but also creates a balanced look along the wall.

174

A wonderful, whimsical idea for storing herbs and spices is to convert an antique dollhouse to a spice rack and hang it on the wall. Each room can hold different kinds of spices for easy access.

Pot racks offer great convenience for getting pots, pans, strainers, and other large utensils out of the way but keeping them within reach. Instead of a standard pot rack, this clever solution uses an old four-rung ladder suspended on chains and equipped with S-hooks for hanging the pots and utensils.

Getting creative with storage can be challenging and fun. Here an old garden gate becomes a pot rack when suspended from the ceiling. The cabinets are flea-market finds fitted and trimmed to do the job of more expensive pieces and the microwave is mounted in an old dresser with its bottom two drawers removed

Gatherers at this country table can make themselves comfortable on an assortment of stools—wood, metal, round or square— all of which store easily underneath.

178

This handsome, custom-built wood-rack snuggly installed above the kitchen sink is a resourceful storage location for frequently used items such as mugs, glasses, plates, and bowls. The different sized compartments, including one to suit a pitcher or vase, makes it even more functional.

179

The pale green frame and burnt orange background of this storage unit showcases a beautiful set of antique red-and-white Staffordshire dinnerware. Simple, festive touches, such as the miniature yews set in the teacups, are all that's needed to incorporate the holidays into your home.

180

You can make a lot of storage out of a little space with open shelves, as this photo shows. The narrow wall between the door and window has two short but deep and sturdy shelves that are the perfect place to stash everyday cookware and tableware as well as a few favorite cookbooks. Beneath, essential utensils hang from hooks attached to the bottom shelf.

181

Painting the cabinetry a warm ocher, similar to the impressive collection of yellowware displayed on the open shelves above the sink, calls attention to the collection yet allows it to become part of its surroundings.

182

Individual open shelves are very simple to install and can be put up anywhere extra storage or display space is needed. Here they exhibit a group of yellowware mixing bowls and pitchers. Hooks below the bottom shelf not only show off charming transferware cups but also reduce the risk of chipping that can occur when cups are stacked.

183

China doesn't always have to be tucked far away in special storage cases. There's something very reassuring about finding cabinets stocked with English china in a set that serves twelve or more. When there's everything from creamers to salad bowls there, a festive dinner party can't be long in the planning.

184

While open shelving does supply a practical storage solution, it can be made integral to the decorating plan as well. Use stenciling or patterned wallpaper to dress up the backs of cabinets and enhance displays of collectibles. The stenciled pattern at the back of this shelf is a variation on the china pattern placed in front of it. Wallpaper is a better solution if the back of the cabinet is uneven, rough, or otherwise unsuitable for that technique.

185

A simple blue cabinet hung against a sunflower-yellow wall can't help but make any country kitchen cheerful. Its pristine white interior is in striking contrast to the distressed finish, and sets off the patterned china and sparkling wine glasses inside.

186

The unfinished pine interior of this blue cupboard creates a delightful contrast to the delicate pink-and-gold-bordered china inside this rustic cabinet. Hanging the elegant double-handled soup bowls gives a homey, cottage feeling and enhances the amusing juxtaposition of styles.

187

Repurpose a plant stand to hold any number of kitchen articles. This tall, black iron one tucked between the fridge and white cabinet holds everyday items.

188

Replace the wood top of an old farmhouse kitchen table with one of polished stone, making it suitable for many tasks, from repotting plants and cutting flowers to prepping meals and dining.

189

True to shaker style, this kitchen is a study in simplicity and order. A unique feature of this serene, white kitchen is the custom storage cabinet on the right—complete with multiple drawers of different sizes for stashing everything from utensils to linens. A series of paneled doors beneath the island/snack bar add additional storage, as does the iron pot rack above.

Decorative iron brackets like these are a nice alternative to more basic ones. They add an unusual and attractive design element. Here, where to store everything has been carefully thought out—with everyday items like glasses, dishware, mugs, and teapots on the lower shelf within easy reach and less frequently used mixing bowls on the top shelf, which gets them out of the way but leaves them accessible.

191

This soft green 1930s-style cabinet with glass-fronted cupboards is ideal to show and store this collection of pale-green glass and ceramics from the period. Mount hooks to make the most use of space, and create an eclectic display.

192

This boxlike grid of open shelving makes a still life of storage areas for glassware, pewter, and ceramics. The combination of clear, reflective, and muted elements, each grouped in its own section, brings even simple objects into sharp focus.

193

Don't hesitate using cabinet organizers for countertop display. This free-standing, open, stainless steel shelf unit is ideal. Strong, lightweight, and versatile, this rack and others like it can be moved to another location or packed away when no longer needed.

194

With plenty of open shelves lining the walls on the right, wall cabinets are not necessary. Instead, items such as pots are hung on a rack, cooking utensils are stowed in a glass jar, and free-standing shelves on the countertops hold everything from mugs to plates.

195

The open shelving in this kitchen has been maximized to display collectibles in a variety of shapes and sizes. The shelving's deep red paint blends with the mahogany stain of the cabinets and makes the collectibles the center of attention.

196

Shallow pine shelves fitted between stud and support columns are a good alternative to deeper, more substantial shelving. These hold everything from mugs, creamers, wine glasses, sugar bowls, and measuring spoons to sieves and books.

197

The spaces in this kitchen are interesting any time of year, but for Christmastime, they acquire a festive air. The blue and white china on the open shelves share space with a forest of miniature Christmas trees and a herd of tiny reindeer.

198

For those who find cabinets with solid fronts boring and glass fronts a little too revealing, gathered fabric may be the answer. The upper cabinets here have a cheerful gingham shirred on their white frames. More gingham appears as a curtain masking the open shelves of the freestanding wooden cabinet.

199

This island contains a good deal of storage built right in. In addition to the cupboards behind the punched-tin doors are top-hinged doors with see-through wire fronts that lift to access produce stored inside. Also a long, narrow drawer is just right for holding knives and other utensils used everyday.

200

Use the often-overlooked space above wall-mounted cabinets to store cook-books, pillar candles, candlesticks, and small kitchen appliances that are used only once in a while. Keep a stepstool nearby to help reach them.

201

With no nearby cabinetry to detract from the immaculate vintage Chambers stove, storage in this corner consists of a bracketed display shelf mounted above a board with hooks holding pots, pans, and colanders. This simple storage treatment and the beadboard paneled walls showcase the stove to the best advantage.

You know a kitchen is seeing a lot of use when utensils and pots and pans are within easy reach for the cook. The long metal bar on this range hood provides a clever storage spot for a variety of tongs and ladles while the professional sized pot rack holds an abundance of cookware.

203

In an active family kitchen, plenty of places to stash things can help the household run smoothly. This kitchen meets this criterion with many well-defined storage spaces. The focal point is the island outfitted with roomy cabinets that hold large bowls and lots of books.

204

A tin watering can is the perfect home for freshly cut flowers. For potted plants, consider a wire container like this to hold a bunch of pots in one place.

There are many ways old-fashioned utilitarian objects can provide storage solutions for modern homes. This wire basket that may have once been used for bringing in eggs from the hen house is now put to good use by holding bottles of mineral water, a modern staple.

Collections of clear vintage jars, bottles, and canisters make great containers to store all sorts of dry ingredients for cooking and baking. Look for them at flea markets, yard sales, and online. Here turquoise-colored canning jars filled with dried beans and grains make a pretty display in this glass-fronted cabinet.

207

Open shelves of different heights in this bright red island are able to hold a variety of kitchen staples, from skinny baking sheets and cupcake pans to a microwave oven and baskets for produce like onions and potatoes.

208

Consider having a refrigerated drawer installed, and, perhaps, a small freezer under a countertop bar for storing mixers, garnishes, etc.

209

On the primitive cupboard in this low-ceilinged room, a collection of white stoneware serving dishes fills the shelves all the way to the beams. Over the stove, shelves holding wooden buckets and containers of cooking utensils also extend to the low ceiling.

210

To preserve work surfaces, cutting boards are often necessary. In this rustic kitchen, those not in use hang from the door, on the wall by the door, and on the side of the cupboard.

211

The stone wall in this kitchen is an attractive feature that needed to be incorporated into the design, not covered up. Open shelves accommodate the aesthetics of the stone while allowing for additional storage space.

212

Large acrylic containers become storage-as-art when filled with foods of different colors, sizes, and shapes, and displayed in open cabinets—especially framed against a fieldstone wall. Everything from grains to breakfast cereals and pastas to snack foods and real fruits can seem larger than life and interesting to look at when stored this way.

213

Black iron drawer pulls recall an earlier era on the drawers and cabinets in this kitchen. Double cabinets with glass-and-muntin doors above the counter and the vintage sideboard converted to an island both supply storage room and contribute to the effect of old-meets-new.

214

Removing the doors on the upper cabinets creates excellent storage and display units that give the kitchen a more spacious feel. Sometimes the things they display are themselves suitable for storage, like the collection of old picnic baskets above the sink. A simple drape on a curtain rod in front of the sink provides privacy for the items stashed behind it.

215

Place fragile plates along a shelf rather than in a large cabinet. Here, even though there is plenty of storage space in this glass cabinet, some white serving pieces reside on a narrow shelf above the stove.

216

Make a new range hood look distressed—like the finish on the surrounding cabinets—by trimming it in wood that's been painted and treated the same way.

217

Screen doors don't have to lead outside. This one hung on the pantry in a vacation home allows greater air circulation to its contents as well.

218

The vintage metal picnic baskets stacked on the floor are fanciful, practical, and quite collectible today. They are excellent storage containers for seasonal and seldom-used things such as Christmas cookie cutters, and, of course they can carry food for picnics and road trips.

219

Converting a vintage pie-safe, originally designed to keep flies off freshly baked pies, to a functional storage piece is simple. Here, it gracefully stores and displays china without requiring any major transformation to the original safe.

220

Keep planters of all shapes and sizes together. This collection of pale green planters is readily available should someone come home with a new plant.

221

Maintain a clean and simple look by keeping colors similar. The above-counter cabinetry here with the frames and muntins of its glass doors painted pale green like the backsplash, mirrors the collection of dishes inside and the vintage containers, scale, and bread box on the countertop below.

222

For a relaxed and informal feel, keep shelves uncrowded. Here, tableware is stored away in other cabinets in the kitchen, with only a few favorite serving pieces on display.

223

Without doors to confine the contents, sturdy open shelving can store quite a lot. To accommodate large round serving plates that don't stack easily, lean them against the wall and place other items in front to ensure that they don't fall forward.

224

Make the most of limited space with functional storage that doubles as a display space. This collection of white ironstone is lovely in its various forms and shapes and should be on show. The plain glass-fronted cabinet houses the entire collection, giving each piece the notice it deserves.

225

Consider incorporating your recycling receptacles into the design scheme of your kitchen. The lower door of this antique cabinet has been removed and attached to a bin on glides, to make a sliding drawer for paper and newspapers, which can be gathered up easily when it's time to take them for recycling.

Hanging shelves free up counter space and do not dominate a wall as a hanging cabinet does. On this counter, round bark-covered boxes hold a variety of small odds and ends.

227

Since every surface can be a useful storage space, consider the value and decorative appeal of baskets. Here, the refrigerator has been built-in to the cabinetry providing a level and stable top for this single picnic basket.

228

Store utensils in a repurposed garden urn rather than cramming them all into a small drawer. Most of the utensils here are wooden, but some wire whisks, a pastry brush, and spoons are also visible. The urn is a refreshing, eye-catching way to keep these kinds of utensils handy.

229

Don't overlook space between cabinets—even in front of a window. This two-tiered wire plate rack suspended by chains can hold dinner and salad plates for twelve or display your collection of vintage china. The bottom of the rack is even with the bottom of the cabinets, which gives continuity of line while the wirework has the appearance of a fretwork valance.

230

This space between the sink and an ordinary storage cabinet is perfect for holding matching baskets. Store everyday items such as dishtowels right next to the sink for convenience.

231

Convert and old serving tray into a charming storage piece for different condiments. The large wooden one here is the perfect place to hold containers of oil, vinegar, mustard, and jams.

232

You can achieve a clean, modern look through a combination of frosted and clear-glass cabinets and the use of open storage areas beneath the sink, range, and island. In-cabinet lighting behind the frosted glass of the uppermost cabinets can suggest sunlight streaming through clerestory windows.

233

An antique cabinet can be slightly reno-
vated to work in your kitchen. This entire
piece has been cleaned, but the distressed
exterior has been kept intact. Inside, some
basic beadboard has been made into a
new back and painted a shade of blue to
highlight the china.

234

Let an antique piece such as this storage cabinet show its age. Use it to display other antique decorative objects like the tole tray and mix in a modern touch such as these glass vases. The hand-lettered sign hung over the latches adds to the charm.

235

A storage container that captures the mood of a kitchen can be equal parts decorative object and practical necessity. Here, both functions are fulfilled by this tall, antique German copper pot, large, useful, and quintessentially at home in this eclectic country setting.

236

Old objects can sometimes be recycled to solve both storage and decorating needs. Here, an antique hamper gets a second life as a side table, providing useful, out-of-sight storage as well as a convenient place to place a lamp.

237

When there aren't any cabinets above the countertop, it is especially important to have storage in the island. This long work area was designed without doors so the open shelves would make sorting, storing, and finding a variety of kitchen items a simple task.

238

To properly store an expanding wine collection, wine refrigerators of all sizes and styles can be installed in a kitchen. This refrigerator-sized unit offers sophisticated, temperature-controlled wine storage.

239

Draw dividers, whether built in or purchased, provide necessary organization for storing silverware. The two-tone handles of this vintage Bakelite set not only complement the natural wood of the drawer's runners but are protected in the distressed-wood dividers that resemble the look of the same period.

240

This piece from the butler's pantry, original to the house, was moved to its new location in the remodeled kitchen, where its divided drawers hold less exalted items than the family silver. The brass hardware, also original, cleaned up beautifully.

241

The small drawers on many vintage cabinets are often divided and make great spots for stashing select items; here, silver knives with pearl handles are stacked in a compartment that's part of a bigger drawer. If silver is to be stored in the drawer, it's a good idea to line the compartments with an anti-tarnish cloth.

Here, a beautiful turn-of-the-century, wide-planked cherrywood sideboard has vertically divided shelves along the bottom, ideal for storing trays and other large objects, such as this collection of Colonial pewter. Table linens, flatware, dishtowels, potholders, and small kitchen tools fit nicely into the row of drawers along the top.

243

Not only is there plenty of storage space in the multitude of cabinets, drawers, and cupboards in this charming kitchen, but it has a nice variety of open spaces, too. Shelves and glass-fronted cabinets help to break up the solid wood door fronts. The cherry cabinetry pulls together the diverse storage pieces and creates a warm and welcoming kitchen.

244

Built-in refrigerator units are a clever way to add storage space to a kitchen. This large refrigerator/freezer with its shiny stainless surface stands out against the white storage unit built around it.

245

The black-and-white checkerboard tiles here make a great backdrop against which to store an eclectic mix of everyday items—especially when they're strategically placed behind the stove where they will see a lot of use.

246

Elegance and timelessness are the qualities that this wet bar space give off. Fitted into one corner of this kitchen, the small wine refrigerator provides storage for wine underneath, while the countertop gives room for other liqueurs on top. The cherrywood, glass-faced cabinets have display lighting—perfect for illuminating a collection of glassware.

247

A small kitchen desk is handy for making lists, paying bills, or keeping up on correspondence. Make it even more functional by removing the drawers to provide storage for magazines.

248

Open shelves can hold a variety of items and still appear neat if the things are placed into jars and containers. Clear glass and labeled containers make identi-fication easy and grouping like containers together will make a pleasing display.

249

Keep an eye out for interesting pieces which you can incorporate into your kitchen. This antique wooden cabinet with a plank door is hung on one side of the window and custom shelves display a variety of eclectic pieces.

250

The need for additional storage can make a little ingenuity go a long way. Try stripping a chandelier of its light fixtures and converting it into a teacup holder, a perfect solution for a cozy nook like this one.

251

Glass-fronted cabinets are ideal for storing items worthy of display. The also provide protection from dirt and dust. This one showcases an extensive collection of vintage printed tablecloths. The primary colors and floral patterns impart a retro feeling to the space.

The charm of this storage space is in the details. Open cubbyholes with undulating surfaces and trim (including carved tassled ends) show off a collection of colorful country linens. The sunflower drawer fronts provide closed storage in a refreshingly unique way.

253

In a small kitchen both storage and design needs can be met at the same time with careful placement of various wall racks. Whether pot racks, spice racks, bakery racks, or plate racks, they all organize and accessorize. Here a plate display rack also has a lower shelf holding a small collection of pitchers and mugs and hooks below for teacups.

254

Construct a pantry from a pair of metal storage shelves. This one is painted blue with individual metal bins taking the place of drawers; labels placed on the shelves help identify the bins' contents. White enamelware, a wire basket of potatoes, and an entire shelf of mineral water break up the geometric pattern of the bins. The large sign painted above the shelves speaks to the country-store feel.

255

Stainless steel countertops and appliances are appropriate complements to the unique metal-on-metal storage unit. Their shiny surfaces seem to pull the light through the glass door and deep into the room.

256

Here, a small space has been cleverly designed to create plenty of storage and display. The owner has assembled a number of pieces of early-twentieth-century kitchen furniture, including the roomy hutch in the background, and painted everything bright white to match the collection of white enamelware utensils and accessories.

257

A clever solution to keeping pans available by the stove is the addition of strong metal coat hooks on the wall. With these, pans can be easily retrieved and replaced while cooking at the stove.

258

Small appliances don't have to take up counter or cabinet space. Drawers that are large and deep like these are big enough to accommodate many small appliances among other things.

259

Repeat distinct design elements to visually enhance the width of a tall unit and physically expand its storage capacity. Here, the style and finish of the modern Hoosier cabinet by the Dutch door is replicated for the cabinets adjacent to the dishwasher.

260

All sorts of things can be used for storage in a large kitchen. Try a quirky corner cabinet like this one to hold an assortment of crockery and mixing bowls.

261

Labeled canisters like these are a great way to store baking supplies and tea or coffee. You may prefer them as a charming alternative to clear ones which display contents for everyone to see.

262

With newly constructed cabinets you can recall an earlier style yet provide all the storage space a modern kitchen needs. The upper set of cupboard doors, with their small windows and contrasting panes, add visual interest as well as extra storage to this kitchen. Even the island is packed with drawers and more cabinets as well as a convenient area for storing bottles of wine.

263

A well-executed design uses every inch of available wall space for work and storage. Floor-to-ceiling cabinetry lends a place for everything, so that nothing is on the countertops that is not being used in the moment.

264

When customizing your cabinets, consider bringing in small drawers instead of traditional bottom cabinets. These can accommodate all sorts of items that shelves within cabinets may not be able to.

265

Finding a convenient yet attractive place to store beverage bottles can be challenging. Water and soda bottles dominate shelf space in the refrigerator while wine racks can commandeer much-needed counter space. A clever solution is to convert a cabinet into a bank of cubbyholes, with slotted bases to prevent rolling, making it the ideal holding area for beverages bottles.

266

A storage idea every wine enthusiast would love is a built-in, temperature-controlled, wine storage area. The designer of this kitchen made sure to include one in an easily reachable spot on the central island.

267

Custom cabinetry can provide a place for everything and lend order to your kitchen when mealtime is over. For example, with the doors closed, these cabinets are attractive pieces of furniture. With them opened, they are functional pieces that house an assortment of appliances.

268

Space shelves with enough room to accommodate large appliances such as the microwave in the middle shelf here and toaster oven below. There is even room on top for large mixing bowls.

269

Corner spaces provide a variety of storage options. Here, open shelves are built into this corner above the sink and hold large white mixing bowls and pitchers.

Glass doors can be etched to reflect different styles. Here, frosted panels with tinted art nouveau motifs and medallions in the center reflect the almost nineteenth-century nautical feel.

271

Make the most of a walk-through kitchen by using all available space. In this design, a large glass-fronted custom-made wall unit with distinctive hardware makes the doors resemble those of old-fashioned refrigerators.

272

Create storage space in novel places. Here, a spindled gallery built into the front of the exhaust hood over the range holds pot lids while hooks attached to the soffit above hold old copper pots and pans.

273

If you love to cook, consider building bookcases around the refrigerator to store all of your cookbooks. The resolution of where to keep them will solve a design issue as well—it will make the appliance less obtrusive.

274

Replace the solid wood door of your pantry with a screened door for a unique look that still separates the storage area from the kitchen but opens up the whole room. The gingerbread fretwork on the door is a pretty touch that adds country charm.

4 appliances

275

Accenting stainless steel appliances with black cabinets as well as a stainless island and stool, give a kitchen a distinctly modern look. However, traditional cabinets like these have an older feeling that works well with antique accessories. The overall effect is one of country-meets-contemporary.

276

Make a kitchen more majestic by adding a La Cornue Château range. Elegant and efficient, it is at home in this rich, country-inspired surrounding. To showcase such a piece, mount a pot-filling faucet and a warming shelf on the stainless backsplash above the range.

277

A large, old-fashioned refrigerator such as this is so compatible with the vintage stove, large double porcelain sink, and other touches that it fits the décor of a country kitchen perfectly.

278

Don't give up on the idea of a large double refrigerator because you are afraid of having to sacrifice storage space. This narrow pullout pantry was designed to roll out from a slender floor-to-ceiling cabinet. The metal shelving units are part of a closet storage system and can be purchased in a number of sizes.

279

All large and small appliances don't have to match. Here, an old Waring blender fits in nicely with the modern dishwasher, stove, and microwave. Vintage and new both work with the timeless quality of these cabinets.

280

Many newer models of dishwashers conceal various setting buttons on top of the door rather than displaying them in a front panel. Consider this when deciding on what features are important to you.

281

If you want to have a cooktop in a center island, don't worry about not having a hood for ventilation—this one has its own down-draft fan, which eliminates the need for a hood and adds to the room's open feeling.

282

A freestanding cooktop on a kitchen island makes cooking for a crowd more fun; you needn't have your back turned on anyone while stirring the sauce. Stools in front offer guests a convenient place to perch and keep the cook company.

283

A white Aga range commands attention—and gets it. Here, it's the central focus of this kitchen and the piece around which the rest of the space is designed.

284

Aga ranges come in an assortment of styles and colors. Although they have a very distinct look, they fit in with many kinds of kitchens.

285

By choosing all white appliances for a white-and-cream kitchen, colorful touches can be applied almost anywhere. Most striking here is the distressed blue farm-house table and chairs, but accessories in red, blue, and yellow also stand out.

286

Small appliances can pick up the established tone of a kitchen. Slightly bluer than the dominant pale green of the room, the turquoise vintage-style toaster works with additional pastel items in the kitchen—particularly the blue bowls on the table.

287

If options are limited, try housing a microwave on the countertop. The open shelves here create a place to house a collection of colorful dishes that might have otherwise been place on the counter.

288

If you are replacing or installing a new dishwasher, be sure to choose one that offers energy and water savings.

289

A white and stainless steel kitchen epitomizes the clean and grand country look. The stainless steel cooktop is mirrored by the fixtures on the white cabinets and by other pieces. Softer touches like the storage baskets and spice jars keep the space clean yet not antiseptic.

290

Rather than have to fill and carry the pots from the range, incorporate a faucet into the backsplash above the stovetop. It will be useful for filling pots with water when needed.

291

Funky, folksy, and functional—this little kitchen has it all. The sage-trimmed gray stove was the modern gas range at the turn of the last century, the pink refrigerator was modern, too—in the 1950s.

292

Pink and gray is a classic fifties combination, and can be picked up in any number of ways to bring the room alive.

293

Hot pink seems an unusual color choice for an espresso maker but when placed beside a pink-rimmed china coffee service, the pairing works beautifully. The intensity of the pink machine is a good match for the strong, chalky blue of the hanging cabinet.

294

These days, the 1940s and 1950s are favorite decades to emulate in décor, and several manufacturers are replicating appliances from that time period in response. If you like retro, your selection of appliances and accessories won't be limited.

295

Some of the more popular colors from the forties and fifties are pink, gray, and green. Here it's pink that prevails in the double ovens and refrigerator.

296

Find ways to fit in small retro accessories in your kitchen—such as the wall-mounted Can-O-Mat can opener and the eggbeater on the counter.

297

While modern ranges may have the newest features, such as modular cook-tops, convection ovens, infrared sensors, and greater energy efficiency, antique and vintage stoves still make for desirable additions to a country house.

298

An oldie, but goodie, this butter yellow 1950s Chambers stove sets the tone for the rest of the kitchen. A collection of enamelware coffeepots above it, and a bright yellow retro stool by the big porcelain sink, all contribute to the look and feel of a mid-twentieth-century kitchen.

299

The classic farmhouse style of this kitchen is defined by the unique range that fits well on the wall between the two large windows.

PAMMER
HOUSE
"HOME AWAY FROM HOME"

300

By placing a cooktop in front of an old hearth, this kitchen benefits from built in storage created on either side of the existing chimney.

301

In a successful mix of history and modern convenience, the spot that once served as the hearth continues to serve as the food preparation area, artfully housing a gas range instead of an open fire and the chimney containing an exhaust system.

302

Stainless steel appliances are timeless elements that work with any style of kitchen. Here, they're paired with Shaker-style cabinets and select antiques.

303

If you are installing a new microwave, consider mounting it on the wall above the stove. Some models have fans which help with ventilation.

304

A narrow kitchen requires you keep the work space highly functional. Here, the microwave has been cleverly tucked under the counter instead of taking up space on top, and the range and sink have been placed directly across from one another, a great convenience for the cook.

305

In a colorful kitchen, appliances, often a neutral element, can join in the fun: the navy enameled range here with cobalt trim complements both the primary-color palette and the vintage look of the cabinets.

306

If the area above your range doesn't lend itself to mounting a microwave, mount it under a wall cabinet in another area. Here, both the range hood and microwave have a place and purpose.

307

White cabinetry and appliances help brighten a kitchen. Integrating warm colors, such as the lemon yellow on the window frame and wall here, will further the effect.

308

A modern refrigerator/freezer, with its collection of magnets intact, can be concealed behind a door in custom cabinetry so as not to interfere with the look of a meticulously designed Colonial American kitchen. Details like period hardware add to the illusion.

309

Style options for appliances are always expanding. Let your refrigerator be part of the cabinetry in your kitchen. When closed, the door and drawers of this refrigerator/freezer are indistinguishable from the surrounding cabinets.

310

Choosing the right handles for your cabinets is important and needs careful consideration. They should be in keeping with the style and proportion of the cabinetry, be easy to grab, and feel strong and secure in the hand.

311

If it's a unified look you like, you may not want to have your appliances stand out from your cabinetry. In this Shaker kitchen, appliances are secreted behind cabinets which are made to look like drawer and cabinet fronts.

312

In an old house that has been lovingly restored you may want to minimize the look of modern appliances as much as possible. If so, select appliances that can be hidden with faux-cabinet fronts. This refrigerator and bottom-drawer freezer are examples.

313

Spotlights installed under wall cabinets come in extremely handy when working at a counter that may not have another source of direct light. This small bar area is the perfect location for a spotlight.

314

Custom-made cabinets can be built to contain appliances of all sizes. Here, the size of the cabinet rivals the impressive double oven and oversized refrigerator/freezer. Details are not lost on this expansive piece either—wide plank construction, tapered feet, and the interesting cornice contribute to the countrified look and mute the metallic finish of modern appliances in the rustic log room.

Stainless steel is a natural choice for a black-and-white kitchen. A clock from the past, with a strong black case and numerals, is right at home above this industrial looking range. It also provides a timer if your chosen appliance does not have one.

316

For those who love the stainless steel look, why stop with appliances? In this contemporary kitchen, the work areas around the sink, including countertops and cabinets, have been finished in stainless steel.

317

Every designer knows the look is in the details. The red chairs and hanging pots are a couple accessories that make the quasi-industrial look of this modern kitchen less edgy and more homey.

318

Utilize a short wall by placing a modern range along it, with just enough space on the side to begin the countertop that extends along an adjoining wall.

319

Black was the color chosen for the appliances in this rustic kitchen because it is most complementary to the stained wood cabinets. Stainless would have felt too cold and white would have taken away from the marble countertops. Black handles on the cabinets link the warm wood to the appliances.

320

Simply adding the latest in stainless steel appliances gives an updated feel to any kitchen space. The gray-tiled backsplash and counters here pick up on the steel coloring, accenting the sleek modern-ness. The light wood cabinets and fresh colors on the chairs and pillows bring in country warmth.

321

Double ovens are a good choice for a busy cook. The chef in this kitchen can bake a turkey and a rib roast at the same time with the pair of wall ovens conveniently placed opposite a counter and prep sink.

322

What to do about the odd space that's typically left between cabinets and the ceiling? Transform it with decorative molding, this simple touch really finishes the room.

323

Choose a stove hood that stands out. This black hood looks almost like a piece of contemporary art. It certainly is the dominant feature in this space.

324

Consider the layout and size of your kitchen when picking out appliances. In another house, these large appliances might seem too big, but here they are dwarfed by the commanding architecture of the room.

325

An in-cabinet wine cellar is the ultimate kitchen accessory for someone who loves wine and/or entertaining. Here, one finds a convenient home beneath a small, round sink of a kitchen bar.

326

Viking ranges appeal to everyone from serious cooks to those who appreciate the aesthetics of their industrial look—their quality and performance are unparalleled.

327

Placing a free-standing range in a kitchen island is a great solution if you like to entertain while you cook—it allows for a free flow of conversation while food preparation is going on. This model is flanked by cherry cabinetry for a classic country look.

328

Sizes of cabinets and appliances should be on a similar scale. This way, large appliances won't dominate and small ones won't get lost.

329

There's no need to worry about mixing modern conveniences with traditional style if the appliances are in keeping with the décor. This sleek refrigerator/freezer is flush with the wall, an option that doesn't sacrifice any floor space. The stainless steel appliances take nothing away from the comfortable feel of this kitchen.

330

In small spaces, efficiency is a primary concern, and efficiency with style is the goal. Here, a countertop cook surface sits over a built-in oven on an extended countertop; the hidden burners provide for a smooth surface, and the white range blends into the cabinetry.

331

Electric cooktops offer enticing alternatives to the more standard gas burners. Cleanup is easier and depending on the countertops—the cooktop can be camouflaged among the surrounding area.

332

A state-of-the-art range takes center-stage in this kitchen. A unique feature is the high-powered hood cleverly hanging above—which displays that a hood doesn't have to be secured to a wall or cabinet, it can also be suspended directly from the ceiling.

5 | sinks

333

Soapstone is a beautiful, natural addition to wood and can be fully integrated into the rustic design of a kitchen. The sink here is constructed of the same soapstone as the surrounding countertops with the apron of the sink left exposed in the farmhouse style.

334

To give a kitchen some individuality, be open to finding alternatives to the traditional sink and tile backsplash. This porcelain sink provides lots of usable work space and is a focal point for the kitchen. It has an integrated backsplash that forms a seamless transition from the sink to the windows.

335

Tasteful brass faucets stand out, gleaming against the white porcelain backsplash of the sink, yet they are completely compatible with the kitchen's pale yellow woodwork.

336

Colonial can meet contemporary as shown in this beautiful kitchen. The color choices and accessories are early American, the cabinet style is country traditional, and the soapstone countertops with a farmhouse sink, are modern. The classic design of the tall, arched faucet works with all styles.

337

A simple thing like a faucet fixture can make a big difference. With such an enormous selection of styles, finishes, and features to choose from, think carefully about what kind of tone you want it to set as well as what you need it to do before selecting and installing one.

338

Sitting as it does between two sets of cabinets, this unique, industrial sink can be approached from either side. Its large size and central location make it an excellent repository for fresh fruits and vegetables that need to be rinsed and prepped before cooking or storing, flowers that need to be cut and arranged, and the 1,001 other uses we create for sinks.

339

The unusual configuration of this cast-iron sink has the faucet coming up the narrow side and countertops cut to support the lips of the sink on opposing sides to create one continuous island.

340

This large porcelain sink, fitted into cabinets that look as if they were rescued from an artist's studio, has the appearance of belonging in an old English country house.

341

Giving cabinets and window casements an age-worn appearance imbues a kitchen with a sense of the past. To further contribute a rural farmhouse look set in place by the large double-sink and rustic cabinets, try soft yellow-colored stucco walls, which can add texture and sunny warmth.

342

Convert an old cabinet or chest of drawers into a sink basin for a unique alternative to traditional matching cabinets or a freestanding unit. This sink area is accented with Victorian prints, old lace, and chandeliers—touches that give this kitchen personality.

343

A large sink located just inside the back door is extremely convenient! This vintage basin is supported by a simple, open wood frame, and has been contemporized by the addition of sleek new fixtures that allow for lots of work space. Elegant yet unobtrusive, this sink earns its keep—while baskets hold items that might normally be kept under it.

344

Without a cabinet below it, the spacious area beneath this sink is the perfect place for small dogs to find privacy when it's time to eat or drink. For the human inhabitants, that means no more accidentally knocking over the water bowl as you're walking around the kitchen.

345

Together, the glass-door cabinets and the abutting double window above the sink create an illusion of a glass wall, giving a sense of openness and light. The space beneath the sink further contributes to this feeling.

346

This long porcelain sink has a lot going for it: first and foremost, its size makes it versatile; its side countertop is also porcelain, making it easy to clean and drain; and its form and color make it an attractive focal point in the kitchen. Room beneath for several napping dogs is available because no shelves were built under it.

347

Don't be afraid to experiment with the unexpected. Here, the addition of a unique aqua sink works to tone down the dominant deep blue color on the walls and floor.

348

The real beauty of a large, cast-iron and porcelain sink like the one is not when it's empty, but when it's full. There isn't a roaster too big or a pot too deep for it to accommodate.

349

A faucet should be both beautiful and extremely useful. One with a high arch allows for cleaning tall and bulky pots. A pull-out spray wand can be used for watering plants, washing a small dog, and to thoroughly clean hard-to-reach places.

350

Instant hot-water faucets and soap dispensers are welcome additions to any updated kitchen. Here, both offer great convenience and complement the ultra modern feel of this space.

351

An island sink is not only an added convenience, but it also makes more efficient use of the work area. When planning your kitchen design, consider options like this. It may be more affordable than you think.

352

Undermounted sinks are exceedingly popular in updated kitchens. They offer easier cleanup because nothing gets caught in the outer edges and work with any type of countertop surface.

353

Choose a restaurant-style brushed-chrome sink to establish an industrial theme along one wall of your kitchen. When flanked by a stainless steel dishwasher and a tall set of painted steel lockers, as well as a set of chrome wall shelves, such a hard-working sink could be in the kitchen of a small café.

354

When renovating your kitchen, let who and where you want to face affect the decision of where to place the sink. Here, the sink is ideally situated for communicating with family and friends during prep and cleanup.

355

A reproduction faucet in a brushed finish lends a timeless quality to this small bar sink, undermounted in a deep blue countertop. Installing the fixture on the backsplash makes countertop cleanup quick. Copies of vintage kitchen hardware are easy to find at most home-supply and plumbing stores.

356

Deep and large, this soapstone sink has an elegant raised bridge faucet so that any work that needs to be done in it is easily managed. For increased functionality, consider adding grooves to the adjoining countertop to form a drain board that spills directly into the sink.

357

A wall-mounted style faucet will allow greater access to the sink than one flush-mounted to the counter, a benefit in a small kitchen.

358

In this poured concrete unit, the sink and countertop are one piece. The wide grooves and gently sloped surface of the drain board make it easy to let dishes air dry without puddles collecting on the countertop. Both poured concrete and stainless steel are materials that make this seamless treatment possible.

359

Place two different sinks side by side instead of one larger one to accommodate different faucets and needs. The sink in the foreground here is slightly lower, with a tall gooseneck faucet made for filling and washing large pots, pails, and buckets. The higher sink is more comfortable for washing dishes.

360

An island with a prep sink, positioned away from the main sink and cooking areas, allows ample room for the cook's helpers. Choose a raised faucet to facilitate jobs like filling vases and tall pots or rinsing large items.

361

A kitchen island is a natural gathering spot for family and friends. With a sink and a few stools added, the area becomes a comfortable place for conversation, doing homework, or for a casual snack.

362

A clever deception fools the eye into thinking this is an old-fashioned, free-standing sink. Extending the sink, countertop, and wooden legs beyond the line of the modern cabinetry can success-fully create this three-dimensional effect.

363

A sink that is part of the countertop and includes a slightly grooved drainage area on which to put a drying rack is an added convenience—it allows the water from just-washed dishes to spill into the sink, making cleanup a breeze.

364

A great way to dress up an old sink is with a new faucet. Many choices are available. This one is practical yet stylish, with an extended spout that makes washing big items easy.

365

Choosing a faucet for a sink or basin is similar to choosing the right accessory to finish an outfit. You want it to complement the style, be attractive yet not ostentatious, and enhance the overall look. The simplicity of this fixture pairs perfectly with the classic tile squares of the sink's backsplash.

A drain board can be custom fitted to your sink. These come in a variety of materials, ranging from polymers to metallics, and can be stored away when not in use.

6 work surfaces

367

Although terra-cotta tiles are usually thought of as floor coverings, they work equally well on countertops. Literally "fired earth," terra-cotta is the most "natural" of all hard tiles. It is easy to clean, ages gracefully to a mellow patina, and the warm orange color and rustic surface is in keeping with a country-style room.

368

Earth-toned granite countertops are a natural extension of the warm wooden cabinets that fill this kitchen. One stainless steel sink is undermounted into the counter and has a small compartment for prep work. The rest of the food preparation takes place on the island because counter space is limited. There, the sink is deep enough to accommodate pots and pans.

369

An oversized hutch can integrate storage and serving space. Here, the newly finished work surface also serves as a buffet. The furniture and the collection seem a comfortable match, in age as well as style.

370

Soapstone has been used in country kitchens for centuries. Its durability and ability to resist stains and not react to acid spills such as lemon juice, vinegar, or wine make it an excellent choice for kitchen work surfaces. Soapstone's warm, natural look and "soft" feel make it an attractive countertop material as well.

371

A large island whose primary purpose is to provide the extra work space needed in a kitchen is a terrific asset! With the variety of materials available today it's easy to put together a look that suits your style—such as the expansive marble work surface here.

372

This kitchen island looks like it is right out of *Alice in Wonderland*, and, in fact, it is in keeping with the whimsical, nothing-is-as-it-seems theme of this kitchen. The basic box shape has been softened by a scalloped bottom edge and curved wood supports the ends in spiral-carved feet; one end of its blue-speckled solid-surface top is a semicircle while the other is an undulating curve.

373

Mounting a small shelf below cabinets frees up a lot of space on the countertop beneath. With baker's ingredients and tools close at hand, the work surface is ready to go to work.

374

A butcher block countertop is a nice partner for modern, steel surfaces. The wood on top of this kitchen's center island softens the coldness of the stainless steel range and countertops that flank it.

375

Countertops of varying heights are extremely helpful when preparing food. Here, the joining of a slightly taller section with one that is shorter leaves ingredients easily accessible to be poured right into the mixer on the lower surface.

376

A unique feature of this large island that houses a sink and dishwasher is the stainless steel top with two grooved drain boards leading to the integral sink. The simple design of only two troughs on each drain board contributes to the sleek look of the surface.

377

Consider silestone composite, a very hard surface almost impervious to heat and water, for countertops. Here, the mirror-smooth surface is unbroken except for the sink and stovetop.

378

The butcher block countertops in this kitchen play the role of great unifier, joining several finishes under one surface: a large, enameled porcelain sink, a white dishwasher, a stainless steel range, and the cabinets beside it.

379

Solid-stone surfaces are attractive in appearance and built to take the punishment of daily life and still look brand new.

380

The elegant-but-easy theme of this kitchen's work surfaces is also applied to the backsplash around the sink area. Practically maintenance-free, the small tiles are grouted with light gray sealant chosen to complement the countertops.

381

Hardwood, stone, or man-made solid-surface countertops offer a number of options for today's kitchens. In addition to the choice of materials, these countertops come in a great assortment of colors and can be cut to any size or shape. Here, a dark blue was chosen for all the work surfaces, including the sink and its apron.

382

A large butcher block makes a practical and durable top to a highly distressed, antique cupboard called into service as an island. Although most of the vertical surfaces in this "shabby chic" kitchen are very rough, the horizontal working surfaces, such as the countertops and floor, are smooth, well finished, and easy to clean.

383

Slate black counters provide a striking visual anchor for a sparkling white kitchen. Add it to a generous island, an ideal place for food preparation which can also function as a breakfast bar or ideally located buffet.

384

Work surfaces have multiple functions—including food preparation or a place to keep track of schedules, invitations, shopping lists, photos, and the other minutia of daily living. This handy combination of a blackboard and a bulletin board makes a perfect "work surface" for these kinds of things.

385

The kitchen is the heart of a family's home, and therefore the best place to set up a family communication center. Hanging a bulletin board, blackboard or both on the wall near a phone makes sense: everyone passes it, sees it, and can pick up or leave messages. It's a great way to keep tabs on each member's comings and goings.

386

In upgrading an older kitchen, make sure to consider how much countertop space suits your needs. This large island offers tons of room for all kinds of food preparation.

387

Achieving a clean look in your kitchen is easier when extensive storage space is incorporated, keeping work areas clear of small appliances and other kitchen paraphernalia.

388

A breakfast bar does double duty as a work surface and eating area. Here, the lower portion serves as a prep station and the higher adjacent portion is ideal for sitting at and eating.

389

The decorative metallic band on the white tile backsplash enlivens the humble gray-granite pattern in the countertop. The finely executed grapevine design adds textural detail to the work surface and a Victorian accent reminiscent of pressed tin ceilings.

390

Perhaps it's instinctual to want to be consistent in the materials chosen for work surfaces, including kitchen countertops and islands. But, it's a good idea to choose different materials to suit the work that's done there: marble for the cooking area and faux-granite for the center island.

391

To the right of the range and window, a group of three open shelves work at holding some commonly used items while freeing up counter space for small appliances at the same time.

392

Careful placement of an island ensures that necessary tools and supplies will always be within reach. The butcher block top of this island provides a large, accessible surface for the many kitchen tasks that need doing.

393

Tiled countertops are an attractive and less expensive alternative than granite and marble. They work well in conjunction with other work surfaces like the butcher block here.

394

This cabinet and countertop enjoy a symbiotic relationship—the cabinet appears to rest on the counter below, while the carved corbels define the work surface, separating it into areas with distinct functions.

395

Convert an old, wooden side table into a versatile work surface, which becomes a chopping block, pastry board, or food prep area as the need arises. A table with no particular value can be stripped of its original finish so as to withstand rough use and cleaning, while still lending pretty lines to a kitchen's charm.

396

Choose butcher block counters for a handsome and hardy work surface. They don't need any special care other than routine cleaning with soap and water and an occasional application of mineral oil to help treat the wood. As with other wood counters, always use a cutting board, as cutting directly on the countertop can damage the surface.

397

If you love natural surfaces, wood and stone are excellent choices. Both come in a variety of shapes, sizes, and patterns. Here, a small, untreated block of stone placed on a wooden cutting board catches any wayward drips of oil or vinegar that could mar the surface of the antique cupboard.

398

Copper countertops provide an elegant kitchen surface that can look old-world or thoroughly modern. This one, which has developed a natural patina and been polished so it gleams, has integral drain boards abutting the sink and tacks that secure it along the rims.

7 windows and lighting

399

Leaving windows bare allows light to enter the room, where it reflects off stainless steel appliances, white cabinets, and glass objects. This is especially useful in a long, narrow kitchen like this one, where some, but not much natural light filters from the double windows above the sink and the windowed door panel.

400

An abundance of natural light can illuminate different collections—such as the various bottles on the windowsill here. Partial shades of unhemmed burlap pick up the warm, rich tones of the wood window frames and allow for a modicum of privacy.

401

Leaded glass insets with stained-glass lozenges add dimension and detail. Here, the combination of unique chandeliers and practical ceiling fans contribute to the eclectic feel.

402

Consider installing French doors in place of windows to let in an enormous amount of light. Here, they lead to the garden and illuminate the small eating area.

403

Light fixtures, whether decorative or practical, should fit in with the style of the room. The flamboyant black-and-white pineapple chandelier above the table is certainly in keeping with the eccentricity of the space.

404

With the sun setting into this bank of windows, the kitchen is awash in gold. The blond wood ceiling and yellow paint add to the glow. When more light is needed, two schoolhouse lights over the sink and an industrial fixture over the island shed light on the work areas.

405

For safety's sake, a night-light is an essential in every kitchen. But don't give up style for utility. In this summer cottage, a small, decorative lamp in the corner of the kitchen counter gives off enough light for late-night foragers.

406

In a large open kitchen and sitting area, glass-paneled double doors may not let in a sufficient amount of light. Using white tiles and lots of stainless steel in the work areas, painting the far walls and slanted ceiling with a light-reflecting paint, and installing clear glass pendant lights above the island are all great solutions to the lack of light.

407

A view like this shouldn't be kept hidden! Without window treatments getting in the way, the full bank of windows and French doors lets the unique ocean view be the focal point of this kitchen.

408

Painting a high-beamed ceiling the same soft color of the walls creates a warm glow in a bright room.

409

Make sure there are sources of natural light all around when designing your kitchen. Casement windows here topped by fixed transoms create a band of additional light just below the ceiling line; a skylight and a glass-paned door bring even more light into the room.

410

When natural light isn't sufficient, recessed lighting in the ceiling fills the bill. In the evening, after the cooking is done and the table is set, chandeliers can provide soft lighting for dinner and conversation.

411

The dining room adjacent to this cottage kitchen is bathed in light, thanks to the French doors opposite the table. When the kitchen door is left open, the light spills in, joining the sunlight from the window reflected in the glass front of the cabinet.

412

Enhance a lone window in a narrow apartment kitchen with sheer curtains and an airy bamboo shade so that little natural light is blocked.

413

The cool, pale blue walls, the white cabinets with glass doors, and the stainless steel appliances reflect the light coming from the one source. After daylight, a single overhead light fixture supplies all the light in this space.

414

Install pendant lights over an island and well-placed ceiling lights to ensure that your kitchen is well lit after the sun goes down and natural light isn't brightening up the space.

415

White walls, ceilings, and floors reflect this bright kitchen's ample supply of natural light. Pendant lighting over the island is simple yet functional; bamboo blinds complement the rich wood finish on the island.

416

Windows all around this kitchen help define it as a light-filled, welcoming space. Placing white tiles on the wall, white cabinets throughout, and maintaining a highly polished floor heightens the brightness, which makes the red accent pieces, particularly the giant red paper roses on the pot rack, explode with color.

417

Backlit by the autumn sun, an orange feather wreath screams "Happy Halloween!" Joined on the windowsill by two black-painted toy fir trees and a white mini pumpkin, this festive tableau invites trick-or-treaters into the kitchen for some holiday goodies.

418

Window treatments can help connect two spaces that are closely related but separate. Here, flat Roman shades of similar striped fabric hang in the small windows behind the sink as well as over the windows in the adjacent sunroom.

419

With natural light coming from two directions and all white reflective surfaces, this kitchen is very bright by day. For specific lighting needs, the height of the pendant lights can be manually adjusted: raised for diffuse light, pulled down for close work.

420

One might suspect that the string of flower-garland colored lights was hung by a child's request. However, when lit at night, the twinkling lights enchant young and old alike.

421

Four large windows placed over the sink and countertop flood this kitchen with light. Daylight can be maximized by having the windows free of any window dressing.

422

Windows aren't always dressed by what's put on top of, over, or around them—they can also be enhanced by something put in front of them. Here, a small stainless steel table, whose top aligns with the bottom pane, becomes part of a dramatic still life when a topiary in an earthenware pot is placed on it to balance the height of the window.

423

French doors, sometimes called French windows, make a graceful transition between indoor and outdoor spaces while flooding the interior room with sunlight and a glorious view. These doors were installed in the exterior wall adjacent to the kitchen, creating an alfresco dining area in summer and an enclosed sunroom when it gets cooler.

424

For a sense of privacy—and a way to incorporate a bit more flounce into the room—consider hanging a three-quarter-length, patterned sheer curtain in the window. The sheer fabric lets light in but obscures the view enough so you don't feel as if you're on stage, especially in the evening when the lights are on.

425

The single window in this small alcove is the perfect backdrop for an eating nook in this cottage kitchen. The simple chrome lamp hanging over the table is operated on a dimmer, allowing the amount of light to be adjusted as needed.

426

Take full advantage of a large, sunny window: transform the space into a bright and inviting breakfast nook by adding a small table and some chairs.

427

When a low-sloping ceiling in the kitchen doesn't leave enough room for full-size windows, skylights are the answer. To make up for the lost window light, they can be installed to put light deep into the room, making what could be a dark kitchen into one that's bright and airy, or to pull in more natural light above the work area.

428

Make use of a number of different light sources. Here, natural light from the big picture windows, a wrought-iron chandelier, and a hanging fixture over the work area all serve different purposes.

429

Sliding glass doors can be closed on a cool day or flung wide to let the summer breezes in. Should the summer sun become too bright, the translucent fabric shades here can be unfurled to cut the glare.

430

One shouldn't compete with the natural beauty of a stunning scene just beyond the windows. Rather, create a living space that is harmonious with nature: bring attention to it by keeping the décor and lighting simple, the color palette neutral, and the seating arranged to take full advantage of the view.

431

Large windows that let in full sun, especially in winter, are a key feature here. Forgoing window treatment allows for maximum light exposure.

432

Light bounces around a room by reflections and refractions off anything from cabinets with glass doors to shiny blond-wood floors and stainless steel appliances. Here, even the chrome toaster and glass jars are part of the lighting effect.

433

Light fixtures can add to a period feeling within your kitchen. This pendant lamp, with its delicate fluted glass shade, is a reproduction of a popular early-twentieth-century style. Even the fabric-wrapped cord of the period is recreated.

434

Stainless casings complement cabinet fixtures and appliances, while cream-colored enamel interiors of the pendant lights here cast a warm glow that enhances all the wood.

435

To control the lighting needed for the various functions in your kitchen, consider having dimmer switches installed so that the lighting can be adjusted accordingly.

436

Position wall sconces to focus attention on something spectacular—such as the soaring cathedral ceiling here.

437

Hanging lights can serve multiple purposes. When the island here is being used for food prep or a quick bite, they ensure that the area is well lit. Whether or not the lights are on, however, they also help define the space, echoing the plane of the island from above.

438

In this kitchen, the soft yellow walls and ceiling absorb the sunlight streaming in and reflect it onto the rich wood, illuminating the space with glints of red and gold.

439

Interior lights added to glass-fronted cabinets are very serviceable. They can highlight a collection, showcase individual pieces, or help to locate things in an instant.

440

Hidden spotlights under the cabinets are an unobtrusive way to light up countertop work areas; they also make excellent night-lights.

441

Choose pendant lights with opaque shades and recessed bulbs for low-glare fixtures that cast light directly where it's needed—in this case, over the two sinks.

442

There's no rule that says you have to stick with the same style or period for each of the light fixtures in a kitchen. Depending on the size of your island and how you want to designate its work surface, you can choose to hang pendant lights of different shapes and different wattages to help differentiate the space, as has been done over this island.

443

One large window at the end of a galley-style kitchen can provide a source of potentially strong natural light. These simple window blinds can adjust the light's intensity as desired.

444

Miniblinds are a simple way to take advantage of light coming in through a window while maintaining privacy. The round café table in this alcove has a brushed-steel finish allowing light to bounce off it and kick up the brightness level of the small space.

445

A mural of a landscape with a far horizon on the wall behind this small sitting area makes the space feel bigger. The colors are soft and warm, and the natural light makes the scene come alive along with the many plants on the windowsill.

446

A few pillows, a blanket in a complementary hue, and the cushioned seat help this corner become a comfy nook for work or reflection.

447

Don't underestimate the difference cabinet hardware can make in a kitchen. The strap hinges and thumb latch handles used here transform the ordinary cabinetry and give it the look of old farmhouse carpentry.

448

Sometimes you can place one thing in a room and entirely change its feeling. The florist's bucket here filled with purple *Allium giganteum* that look like they're out of a Dr. Seuss book infuses the kitchen with whimsical energy that plays off the vibrant folk colors of the painted tool caddy.

449

Remove upper cabinet doors so that the shelves can serve as showcases for collectibles rather than spaces where things are put away and kept out of sight. The variety of items in this rustic kitchen suggests an eclecticism that is carried over to the kitchen table, itself an antique surrounded by mix-and-match chairs.

450

If you want to display accessories that don't fit well on a shelf, secure them on the wall instead. The vintage painting tools here would have gotten lost among all the larger items on these shelves, making the wall above the sink an ideal place to hang them.

451

Rich wood grain glows from the walls and work surfaces of this bright, cozy kitchen. The woodwork provides a remarkable backdrop for the autumnal leaves and berries and the late-fall ornamental cabbage on display in the arrangement.

One wonderful find at a flea market can give your kitchen a fresh, new look and make you feel good. This lovely old earthenware vase filled with summer wildflowers accomplishes both these things.

453

Assemble objects from a time period you love—such the Colonial tin chandelier over the table here which is lit by candle-power, not electricity.

454

Transform a space with the right placement of select pieces. It's important to balance verticals and horizontals as well as color and texture for a harmonious appearance, as this arrangement shows.

455

This chalkboard message center is not tacked to the wall but built into the kitchen cabinetry, ensuring that it will always be right where it is needed. Its location on the front of the pantry is the ideal spot for jotting shopping lists, reminders, and messages.

456

Seek out hardware that is as functional as it is attractive; it should last and last. The antique—yet durable—hinges and latches on this cherrywood cabinet are truly striking. The steel against the cherrywood makes the contrast of materials particularly noticeable, each one standing out more sharply together than they would alone.

457

Research is essential when striving for realism in creating a period kitchen. This custom-built kitchen in an 1840s saltbox is full of authentic details. The cabinets have raised panels and beaded edges; the sink and countertops are soapstone, often used by nineteenth-century New Englanders.

458

Antiques contribute to the re-creation of the period, especially the tall walnut cupboard, the small chest of spice drawers, and the old worktable and bench.

459

What a painting for a country kitchen! Why not? There's a place for wit and humor everywhere—even in the kitchen. On a white wall above a chest of drawers, this painting commands attention.

460

Fundamental to a love of flea market and antique store finds is the ability to put the variety of pieces you've collected over the years together attractively. This kitchen reflects an eclectic mix of items from the 1930s, 40s, and 50s that together establish a cheerful retro look.

461

Carefully choose objects to bring certain eras to life. Some great diner stools here accompany an old wooden farmhouse table. A green breadbox sits atop the fridge and an old ceramic pitcher, blue glass cake stand, and antique miniature yellow cabinet share the top of the vintage dish cupboard.

462

The changing seasons are great times to bring out your favorite seasonal objects, such as this collection of vintage flatware with colorful Bakelite handles that echo the shades of autumn leaves. Using these pieces only on occasion—for Thanksgiving dinner, for example—makes them extra special.

463

Compose your own still life by juxtaposing a photo, painting, poster, or other graphic representation with one or more common household items with a visual or functional connection. Here, an oil painting featuring a cup and saucer shares counter space with crockery jars and their contents.

464

When common kitchen utensils are stored together, the tall ones inevitably block the way of, or become tangled up with, the smaller ones. In this kitchen, the height problem has been solved by using three pitchers, all the same style but in three different sizes, to store large, medium, and short utensils.

465

Antique bone- or ivory-handled utensils are great to have on hand when friends of family drop by for dessert. They add a touch of simple elegance to the occasion and make guests feel special, so that even if the visit is a brief one, it can be especially memorable.

466

Bringing out some well-loved china or vintage silverware for coffee and pie can make having a simple snack in the kitchen into an experience. These antique silver forks have bone handles; a delight both to eat with and hold.

467

Collections of distinct vintage pieces are perfect for setting a one of a kind table—such as this holiday dessert table starring an assortment of vintage milk glass.

468

Antique glass bottles make unique vases. Their various shapes, sizes, and colors are perfect for decorating a kitchen windowsill. Fill them with fresh flowers, freshly cut herbs, decorative branches or simply leave them empty and let the light shine through them.

469

Marrying the old and the new is done masterfully in this kitchen. The flat-screen LED television clearly put this kitchen in the now. Yet, an antique wooden bench, chairs, and large cupboard add elements found in kitchens of earlier times.

470

If you're going to choose a dramatic black-and-white scheme for your kitchen, accentuate the drama with pieces that are equally bold. The black serving dish with a white arm reaching across is from Fornasetti and definitely stands out. In front of it, the clear glass chemist's beakers, now measuring cups, are also unusual.

471

It's been said that two similar items start a collection; three or more make a collection. In a quiet corner of this kitchen, established and new collections gather— making it easy to mix and match both.

472

A few lemons and a plant are all that's needed to add zest to a basically neutral tableau—they add refreshing splashes of nature's colors that warm up the scene.

473

An assortment of wire kitchen utensils, old, new, and handcrafted, makes a whimsical window treatment that is reminiscent of the work of Alexander Calder. The artist, though famous for his playful mobiles and sculptures, often sat in his kitchen making practical utensils of twisted wire while his wife cooked dinner.

474

When it comes to kitchen decoration, deciding what works and what doesn't can take time. Here, harmony is established by arranging pieces from collections of similarly colored pottery in different parts of the room so as to draw the eye from place to place, focusing attention on each arrangement rather than the entire collection.

475

A basic white theme provides a ready canvas for decorating during any of the seasons and special occasions. Here, orange and black touches are introduced in anticipation of Halloween.

476

With high ceilings in the kitchen, open shelves can be positioned with plenty of room between them so that they can accommodate items of various sizes as well as keep the area feeling spacious and uncrowded.

477

If you are going to decorate the house for a holiday, don't forget to decorate the kitchen. This Halloween display—featuring a variety of treats and kitchen accessories like a vintage apothecary bottle—will have goblins of all ages gathered around it.

478

Look for imaginative, new uses for single-purpose items so that they will be in service more often and in nontraditional places. Here, a garden stand designed to hold potted plants is used in the kitchen as a makeshift caddy and centerpiece for a fall party, holding flowers, plates, silverware, the sugar bowl and a pumpkin pie.

479

Since food is an important part of holiday celebrations, save some home-baked Christmas cookies to decorate your kitchen. Sparsely elegant, these hand-made tinsel Christmas trees are little works of art with star-shaped cookies-turned-ornaments.

480

Beautiful pieces like these vintage green mixing bowls can help define the palette of a room. Be careful to make color choices that will complement the pieces that you really love so you will want to display and use them rather than stash them away.

481

A selection of retro enamelware in similar or different colors can make a modern kitchen feel homier. Here, an old coffeepot, bread box, and colander bring some old-fashioned charm to a sleek, stylized space.

482

It is considered good feng shui to fill a bowl-shaped object on display; in this case, the gourds in the colander should bring luck.

483

If you're devoted to a certain period or style, you may want to go all out in the details. Pink and gray are the signature colors of this 1950s-looking kitchen, which are reflected even in the choice of paper napkins, chrome holder, and stainless salt and pepper shakers.

484

Silver can always be counted on to dress things up and what can be a more evocative color to display it against than Tiffany blue. You can often find wonderful silver objects at flea markets and antique shops.

485

What might have been a more traditional kitchen got a refreshing facelift with this nautically themed design—exemplified by the blue-and-white colors, large shell tiles, and ship painting.

486

With blackboard paint, you can easily transform almost any space into a functional family message center. Apply the paint to a smooth, flat wooden surface of whatever size you want or need, then frame it to your liking. A blackboard is a fun surface for family members to share news and notes.

487

Hang a small gallery shelf directly beneath a small wall cabinet to create the perfect place to store spices. It keeps them lined up neatly and clearly visible. And upper shelves remain handy for everyday items like mugs and bowls.

488

Expanding collections and unique flea-market finds are, sadly, often stashed away. Not here, where open cabinets and plenty of shelves keep well-loved objects on display and within reach. Some of the treasures include silver and pewter barware, Mason jars, mixing bowls, and linens. In this kitchen, more is, definitely, more.

489

Don't hesitate to use a combination of colors to display several collections to their best advantage. Here, deep rose cabinet interiors showcase the primarily white export china while the kitchen's pale blue walls set off the group of black trays over the mantle.

490

The art deco styling and bold, bright colors of Fiesta dinnerware have kept it as popular as ever since its introduction to American households in 1936. Piled high and alongside other brightly colored pottery pieces, it creates a dazzling display.

491

Shiny white bowls and pitchers are classic country kitchen accessories, whether displayed on their own or in groups, with items like flowers or utensils inside them. These are empty, but when paired with antique canisters against a backdrop of tan tiles and the wood window frame they form a simple and serene picture of cottage life.

492

Use one collection to support another: these three old mismatched pitchers hold an equally mismatched collection of flatware. The small cut-glass creamer holds silver and stainless; the other two hold an assortment with handles of Bakelite, ivory, bone, horn, and wood.

493

Thanks to old treasures found at flea markets and yard sales, this kitchen is like a step back in time—covers of cookbooks from the 1950s and 60s are worthy of prominent display.

494

Display many of your favorite pieces by getting them off your work space. Stretching across the wall above the windows here is a long shelf that holds a collection of white ironstone pitchers.

495

Nothing can substitute for a conveniently placed trash can. This one-time laundry hamper beside the island was roughly painted to allow the former color to show through and given a new home and job in the kitchen.

496

Mix continents, eras, and design styles for surprising harmony—even in a country kitchen. You'll find that traveling not only broadens the mind, it also can broaden one's decorating possibilities.

497

This life-sized replica of the "Sworded General," one of the terra-cotta figures that guard the emperor's tomb in Xi'an, China, protects his new home from the corner of the kitchen. Here, his gaze falls past the stainless steel appliances and onto an ornately carved, marble-topped Victorian table, now used as an island. An iron chandelier with pagoda-shaped shades hangs from the beamed ceiling in yet another juxtaposition of cultures.

498

Open-style kitchens are becoming the norm and the line between the space for food preparation and for gathering to share food is disappearing. A nice middle ground—such as this half wall—separates the kitchen from the dining area.

499

Welcome everywhere in the home, and especially on the table, flowers add color and fragrance. Here, a tall tropical plant brings life to the table while a trailing plant extends along the top and down the side of a cabinet.

500

Play with simple items to create interesting arrangements. Each piece in this white ceramic breakfast set does double duty. The milk pitcher makes a great vase for blood-red roses; egg cups can also be used as mini vases; and a pedestal serving dish needs only yummy baked goods on it to look fantastic.

photo credits

Page 393: Gridley & Graves
Page 394–395: Keith Scott Morton
Page 396–397: Jonn Coolidge
Page 397: Keith Scott Morton
Page 398: Steven Randazzo
Page 399: Steven Randazzo
Page 400–401: Keith Scott Morton
Page 402: Steven Randazzo
Page 403: Steven Randazzo
Page 404: Michael Luppino
Page 405: Keith Scott Morton
Page 406–407: Keith Scott Morton
Page 408: Keith Scott Morton
Page 409: Keith Scott Morton
Page 410–411: William P. Steele
Page 412: William P. Steele
Page 413: Keith Scott Morton
Page 414: Keith Scott Morton

Page 415: Keith Scott Morton
Page 416–417: Keith Scott Morton
Page 418: Keith Scott Morton
Page 419: Keith Scott Morton
Page 420–421: Keith Scott Morton
Page 422: William P. Steele
Page 423: Keith Scott Morton
Page 424–425: Jessie Walker
Page 426: Gridley & Graves
Page 427: Gridley & Graves
Page 428–429: Steven Randazzo
Page 430: Michael Luppino
Page 431: William P. Steele
Page 432: Keith Scott Morton
Page 433: William P. Steele
Page 434: William P. Steele
Page 435: Keith Scott Morton
Page 436–437: Philip Clayton-Thompson

Page 438: Keith Scott Morton
Page 439: Charles Maraia
Page 440: Jessie Walker
Page 441: Keith Scott Morton
Page 442: Steven Randazzo
Page 443: Steven Randazzo
Page 444: Janice Nicolay
Page 445: Gridley & Graves
Page 446–447: Gridley & Graves
Page 447: Keith Scott Morton
Page 448: Keith Scott Morton
Page 449: Jonn Coolidge
Page 450: Keith Scott Morton
Page 451: Keith Scott Morton
Page 452: Keith Scott Morton
Page 453: Keith Scott Morton
Page 454: Keith Scott Morton
Page 455: Ann Stratton

Page 456: William P. Steele
Page 457: William P. Steele
Page 458: Ray Kachatorian
Page 459: Charles Schiller
Page 460: Keith Scott Morton
Page 461: Keith Scott Morton
Page 462–463: Grey Crawford
Page 464: Keith Scott Morton
Page 465: Keith Scott Morton
Page 466 (left): Robert Kent
Page 466 (right): Keith Scott Morton
Page 467: Michael Luppino
Page 468: Michael Luppino
Page 469: Keith Scott Morton
Page 470–471: William P. Steele
Page 472: Ray Kachatorian
Page 473: Keith Scott Morton

index